SIMILITUDE

§

GRANT HIER

www.pelekinesis.com

Similitude by Grant Hier

ISBN: 978-1-938349-98-0

eISBN: 978-1-938349-99-7

Library of Congress Control Number: 2018041517

Copyright © 2018 Grant Hier

This work is licensed under the Creative Commons Attribution-NonCommercial-NoDerivatives 4.0 International License. To view a copy of this license, visit http://creativecommons.org/licenses/by-nc-nd/4.0/.

Cover artwork: Grant Hier

Layout and book design by Mark Givens and Grant Hier

First Pelekinesis Printing 2018

For information:
Pelekinesis, 112 Harvard Ave #65, Claremont, CA 91711 USA

www.pelekinesis.com

SIMILITUDE

poems by
Grant Hier

For all of my teachers.

Ancient Greek ὥρα hṓra ("time, hour") →
horos ("marking stones") →
horizein "divide" →
aphorizein ("aphorism"): apo ("from") +
horizein ("to bound")

CONTENTS

PART I:
FROM DIVIDING

Single Cells

The Story and Morning Grow Lighter	19
Threnody	20
Navigation	21
Naturally	22

To Anaphase

Across the Town	26
Along the Wild	27
Where Dreams Meet Reality	28
There Waking Lost the Lie	29
Morning Attendance	30
Evening Inventory	32
Wildland Fire	34
Ashes, Ashes	35
What We Don't Know of Confusion	38
What You Know of Clarity	39
Key Adjustments	40
Maladjusted	41
Self-Similar	42
Self-Similarity	43
Reunion	44

Departure	45
Paid	46
Spent	47
Disbelief's Long Humming	48
Sentiment Like Lacebark	49
Belief Systems	50
Relief	51
His Wonder Was Our Clear Midnight	52
My Waking Was My Wading In	53

To Cytokinesis

play time	57
Primary Colors	59
A Life	60
Somnambulism and Sleep	61
The Woman Who Paints Hearts on Stones	63
Because the sky was soft and slow	65
Should They Ask Her Name	66
Half of the World is Always in Darkness	67
The Woman Crushed by the School Now Rubble	68
End-of-the-Month Ritual	71
Overtime	72
Charity	73
Gardening as Self-Help	74
Waiting for the Music to Resume	75
Eating a Plum in the Dark	77
X	79

To Synthesis

what doesn't find the center finds the shadow	85
The Sameness Changing	86
The Wax Buddha Melts into Slumber	87
[...more at CHANCE]	88
What Then is Seen	89
Unforeseen Consequences	91
Once He Thought He Changed	92
For Now	93
Of Flight and Communion	95
Levels of Smell	96
Levels of Noise	98
Levels of Sight	100

To Organisms

Femme Fatale as Applied to Food	105
Coincidences	106
The Weakness We Take From Ourselves	107
The Night That Unites Us	108
Not Tired	109
Burning Crops	110
Comfort for the One Who Waits in Patience	111
Nighthawks and Dawn Chorus	113
All-Encompassing	114
Pouring Water from a Larger Vessel into a Smaller Vessel	117
Bestowal	118

All, all alike	119
Fallings-Out While Dressing	120
Then I will roll again with them	121

PART II:
FROM THE HORIZON

To the Ocean's Daughter

Before the Poet Went to Bed	129
In Praise of Slow and Silent Growth	130
I Heard Something Singing	131
Muse Gaze	132
Watermark Angels	134
I Must Sing	135
After Light	136

PART III:
FROM A SERIES
OF MARKING STONES: APHORISMS, ANALOGIES, AND OBSERVATIONS

To

From a Series of Marking Stones: To	143

When You

From a Series of Marking Stones: When You	147

When We

From a Series of Marking Stones: When We   153

You Are

From a Series of Marking Stones: You Are   157

What

From a Series of Marking Stones: What   161

As

From a Series of Marking Stones: As   165

Bound

From a Series of Marking Stones: Bound   169

Acknowledgments   193
About the Author   195

PART I:
FROM DIVIDING

SINGLE CELLS

THE STORY AND MORNING GROW LIGHTER

Earth eases us
to newness
each dawn.

Each duskfall as
well, through this
life drawn

out breath by breath,
light through us
reborn.

THRENODY

Again we see
no gain: seaweed
threads across
tidelines, the same
old story retold
over the same
sand—shorelines
that have yet to be
transcribed
from the longhand
scribble
the moon leaves us.

NAVIGATION

New lines drawn
point by point
(that point to new
directions,

implications,
and assumptions)
may save time
or lead to more

detours—or
to red herrings.
Best to re-check
your bearings.

NATURALLY

The rhythms of the earth are hard to learn
when one stays indoors
for too long. Seasons slowly turn
in sun or ice.
Of course,

it's difficult to see the increments—
as in the mirror
your face grows slightly different
each day. Nothing
clearer.

To Anaphase

ACROSS THE TOWN

Bell splashes awake.
Waves pulse the sky to vibrate
all flesh near, each leaf
hung—the tone, transposed, hums now
within, drives both sap and blood.

Traffic floods the roads
before work, at noon, at five.
Cars take turns merging,
regardless of each driver's
religion or politics.

The waitress takes home
the newspaper left behind
in the booth. Kicks off
her shoes that night. Feels the toll.
Solves the puzzle. Curls her hair.

Mourning doves rest like
notes on the same power line
the scavenger rat
ran all last night. Lights change. We
find a way to share this world.

ALONG THE WILD

Creek splashes. Snake track
waves pulse the sandy banks with
fresh patterns. Each note
sung here. Bones exposed from snow
melt. The hives will hum here soon.

Havoc of roadkills
punctuate the blacktop. Life
has no rehearsal.
Cars reflect the drivers' grief,
collisions' verses.

We wait for the one
who's patient and kind, but in
truth, we fight. We scoff
at gentleness. Seek to find
hardness within. Curse the weak.

Worker bees protect
the queen in winter, her fine
piping. They cluster,
flutter to keep her warm. We
find a way to bear this world.

WHERE DREAMS MEET REALITY

The sky was such
we could not tell
at which point
it touched the earth.
Such confusion
was a blessing—
though it could have been a curse,
we could not tell.
Such confusion.
We touched the earth,
as which point
the sky was such
a blessing—
though it could have been a curse.

THERE WAKING LOST THE LIE

The ground was not
much reassurance,
soft and banking underfoot.
You could stay silent
like the dew and frost.
Glances out the window
for what was lost by dream's end,

and by the time
you would decide
to rise, avoidance
of light outside
brought clarity—
the curse of
knowing how much sky.

I avoided
the morning.
Later, the earth
criticized by burning
the answer through
bare feet at noon.
Late start, though it could have been worse.

MORNING ATTENDANCE

A lecture hall packed: one thousand
eyes. Jackets and hoodies a patchwork quilt
when seen from the back. From the front
it looks more like a rumpled pajama party.
Yet each outfit was selected by each
one there to adorn and protect.

Across the campus, the teachers' lounge
is strewn with boxes, bags, and totes
to carry and secure folders
of paper: dried ink holding
exhausted thoughts and old quotes,
re-purposed. One jacket drapes a chair.

The parking lot is strewn with trash:
candy wrappers, pen caps,
chip bags whose silver linings
glint like broken glass, and broken
glass. Inside of idling cars,
late students waiting for spaces.

On the freeway more cars stopped.
Each one a box to impress, protect
from rain and other dangers. Drivers
sport the outfits they selected
appropriate for their concerns:
to impress, to protect, to warm, to adorn.

Built atop the surrounding hills,
houses likewise built to protect
and impress, but unseen within: papers,

rumpled sleepers, family heirlooms,
coats, hats, glasses, spectacles,
trash, and more cars waiting.

In the open spaces outside of the city:
windbreakers of eucalyptus, tails
of birds flashing colors to impress,
topcoats of soil protecting new seeds,
the powdered coats of blueberries
speckle a fence of wet wood.

One thousand miles north, muck
boots on a porch. Wet fleece
of sheep. Glossy cloaks of plump
blackberries. An orchard full of plums
dripping with rainwater, each orb
an eye reflecting Mount Hood.

EVENING INVENTORY

One thousand miles north of here,
cloud cover smudges the moon.
From above, Mt. Hood appears
as a star: snow and gray volcanic ash
radiating, even as dusk flattens all to
monochrome gray on the way to black.

On the drive back home, coastal
madrones and redwoods silhouette
against the Pacific. The cold air, near
saturation, turns to fog, while out in
the heaving surf, boulders erode to
sand. Becoming less still. Becoming silt.

Cutting inland, tule fog blurs the edge
of sky and ground. And silt here, too,
from when the central valley floor was seabed.
Deep beneath the misty rows of olive trees
then: whale bones, shells, redwood chunks
decomposing. Decomposed.

In the Mojave, seventy-seven almonds
on a single tree, lit by a porch light
turned on too early, each pod
glowing like the green beetles
orbiting the corrugated shells.
The Earth's steady spin to evening.

Under the eaves of suburban homes
caterpillars cling, cocoon themselves
to become liquid before becoming new.

All things rearranged along the way.
Between here and there. Between what
we had planned, and what has become.

WILDLAND FIRE

The foothills appear to awaken.
Subterranean roots smolder. Wisps
of smoke at first, then yellow and red fringes
as the dried scrub ignites. A snaking line
of orange crawls unimpeded. The wind gusts,
sends the fire front up the hill, over the ridge,
racing toward the roads, toward the homes.

Soon the range sends up thick veils of gray,
rising tunnels of black that tumble and billow.

Helicopters appear quickly,
hover in the clearer skies
around the glowing show,
streaming live news feeds
to their home stations.
As the blaze grows, more
choppers circle like flies.

Cell phone towers overload. Garden hoses
send futile arcing streams up onto the roofs.

Doors to cars and homes are left open
as boxes are shuffled out. People shout,
hug quickly. The wild animals have already fled
ahead of the mandatory evacuation orders.
Horses are led onto trailers. Dogs are carried
into cars. Names of cats are called over and over
again into the swirling embers of the night.

ASHES, ASHES

The city may seem asleep on the streets
but parties on rooftops bounce light off low clouds.
Skyscraper fires will do the same.
Rooftops may blare or blaze.

The way may seem safe from dangers, and we
may startle ourselves with our worrying ways.
Warnings beforehand may shock or annoy.
Alarms may scare or save.

We cover our eyes with our hands at the thought,
and peep through our fingers to soften the fear.
Hope can persuade us to be brave.
Lace will filter the view of graves.

The fires may rage somewhere far away,
but in the cool morning the sharp smell of smoke
pierces the day. You're safe here. Still,
a haze of black remains.

Rooftops may blare
or blaze. Alarms may
scare or save. Lace
will filter the view
of graves. A haze
of black remains.

suppositions
of the
refugee

how expectation leans	how the night learns	now reflection turns
on the day disburses	of the dawn's sure coming	a new lens on the seasons
light becoming form	encouragement from	reversals of plans
as it embraces	birds that trace this	concerns of reluctant
all it encounters	uncertainty of returning	migrations and displacement

meditations
on the
mediators

now excavation awaits	now explanations wait	now exploration creates
redundant recursive	incumbent on learning	abundance returning
fields of rows	even though	wonder through
within rows of fields	uneven we know	more wonder and so
in fractal landscapes	a map can take shape	the practice expands

WHAT WE DON'T KNOW OF CONFUSION

Is how confusion reigns.
It becomes apparent

through the understanding.
Is seldom the same as

what we envisioned
underlying what

we don't know.
What we don't know

becomes apparent
from the trying.

Becomes apparent
in the failures of the day.

These things
will disappear

as the mist does
after morning.

We calculate our fears
without fair warning.

WHAT YOU KNOW OF CLARITY

Isn't how clarity blurs.
What muddies

in our confused state
is always different.

What you forgot
on top of that,

what you know,
what you knew,

becomes jumbled
by not applying yourself.

Becomes unclear
through successes.

Revelations
may appear

as the breeze does
before nightfall.

You estimate your strength
by sabotage.

KEY ADJUSTMENTS

The old ukulele
tries to stay in tune,
its pegs slipping,
friction determining
hold. The strings
are old (like its
owner, who bought
it new)—not as bright.
True, but still able to
make a joyous noise
when tickled by
the things of this
world. Still able to
hold tension, too.

But fine instruments,
like clocks (like us)
wind down. Time changes
things. Perhaps starting
with less expectation—
of what it once could do,
say. One whole step down
from 440 "A" works
okay. Tune it there,
to "G" instead: What
its owner says when
stepping down the one
step in route to check
the mailbox: "Gee…"

MALADJUSTED

The young drummer
surrenders to the noise,
guitar feedback
binding, resisting—
chance notes released.
No key. The guitarist
is young, too (like
his instrument).
Shiny beyond polish.
Not dull. But unable
to make a joyous noise
when so pissed off
at the world. Unable
to get the attention.

But punk is all
about the anger, with no
consolation. What can
the young do, say,
with a limping world to
inherit, already wound
down to half its beauty?
Already spent. And they
are supposed to feel— what?
Indebted? No. Rock and roll.
Trash the room. Crack
the neck against the amp
until nothing in the place
can stand the tension.

SELF-SIMILAR

Folds of the bath towel strewn on the floor
echo
folds of mountain ranges reaching to our north.

Fanning of silt ridges in the river mouth delta
parallel
fanning of sands in arroyos
carving the drier hillsides to our south.

The familiar fractals of knuckle wrinkles
spanning the back of your hand tonight
echo
the strange York Gum burl at the farthest west
patch of the Wheatbelt lands in Western Australia.

The small slub lumps of unraveling across the woolen yarn
parallel
the scratchy rows of tremors from the east
on the seismogram.

Grief of the woman I've never met, crumpled
wailing in the dark
creases my brow in the shape of our borders
the force of the blow
the source of pain.

SELF-SIMILARITY

Spray shape of a dendrite branching—
of bifurcation in a Mandelbrot set,
of slime mold in a freshwater tank,
electron beams streaming through acrylic blocks,
bonsai branches in a garden sky,
bronchial tree of a human lung,
Lichtenberg figures burned across flesh,
brown rivers forking in desert mud,

canals on Mars—
the fusion paths in stars.

Shape of a brain neuron splaying—
the tiny crack in the lip of a crystal glass,
a fissure embedded in greenish pond ice,
a rootball mesh in wet black soil,
a mortar burst,
a firework—
path of the gas expansion in a crab nebula after a supernova.

Swirl of mystery in pupa darkness—
of your bathwater down the drain—

whorl of spiral galaxy to black hole,
emerging as a fountain of light out the other side.

REUNION

On days the mornings
open themselves,

we open our eyes
alert,

as if awake for hours.
Refreshed,

we open the covers,
wash,

open the paper,
open the Internet

to see what
others see—

open our arms
to the world

as if we
are embracing

a loved one
returning,

as if asking
forgiveness

from the day
for ever sleeping

or turning
away.

DEPARTURE

Nights the evenings
bind us.

We close our mouths,
tired,

as if sleep shuts
down speech first.

We close the shutters—
darker—

close the book,
click the lamp

to make all things
equally dark—

fold our legs
beneath us

as if embryonic poses
protect us

from what comes
once we turn to sleep—

or we crouch
as if ready to run

with the first
awakening,

the return
of the day.

PAID

Enlivened ennui,
so I sing as I soar
through the first seconds
after rising, as I rushed
later out of my driveway,

the short, sweet flight
away, full tank, fresh start.
I open my windows, wind
cold like metal, calming
the first doubt that's never right.

SPENT

Deadened energies
so I'm silent as I coast
through the last hours
before bed, as I coasted
before into my driveway,

the long, grueling drive
home on fumes finally done.
I pinch my nose, eyes
hot like my engine, burning
the last of whatever's left.

DISBELIEF'S LONG HUMMING

Unraveled by pastels
of sunset easing to
dusk, leaving tops of wet
stones duller with each breath,
a slow turning away,
the wealth of stillness now
a wholeness within us.

Roundness of full moon tests
the straight line of the lamp
post's shadow across its
own circle of amber
throw: sidewalk clock face and
one moon-shadow hour
hand measuring the night.

Easy to forget our
shallow skimming of small
talk, lost second-hand news
and conversations not
worth saving. The wafers
placed on the plate, unclaimed.
Discs stacked on the spindle.

SENTIMENT LIKE LACEBARK

Tangled in the dim glow
of street lamp dappled through
gauze trees, it is as if
we are surfacing from
a deep dive, starved for breath,
a fisherman's net cast
overhead between us
and the fractured surface.

Sickle of dusk's harvest,
the crescent moon sliver
a fish hook suspended
as if to catch the first
of twilight's migrations.

Difficult to know if
our deep wading through new
communion, these weaving
lines, will capture or free
us, tides of unknowing
reversed to expose strange
shells and starfish in blue
tide pools of becoming.

BELIEF SYSTEMS

What was misunderstood—in the long strain of winter's
emergence to green from blue ice and stiff stems—
becomes apparent in the revelation of the new
bud, quivering at the end of the twig now,
shaking a drop loose to the same wind
that shook them both when they
clung together before thaw.

That we christen cold steel with chilled champagne,
enter allegiance with things that hold us up—
bridges and buildings appearing where
there were wide open skies—there
we take note, make speeches in
rituals, look to both pain
and healing as law.

Not that what was understood was irreversible.
Not that we failed to understand what we
failed to achieve—the failures of our
execution of the blueprints we
took seasons to plan, draw
from the light, convert
to height, stand upon.

Constitution loses form. Human nature reverses
expectations once it is known that the goal
is beyond reach. Apathy sets in as the leaf
is threatened by the stem's stiffening.
Now that the wind is increasing in
stages again—now that the ice
is blue—we will stand down.

RELIEF

What is known—in the short crease of summer's
easing to cooler winds from light blue skies—
disguises the amnesia of those older
blooms, quaking at the dry ends,
clinging to drops, loosening
in the gusts then, still
proud before the fall.

That we listen to what is told by the campaigns
of winter, exit without things we once held
up as true, is what saves us in the end.
Winds sting as if wet, colder than
reflections in blue ice—here,
nothing saves the warm
trust of shared breath.

Not that anything or any season lasts. It can't.
It is designed to make us weep. Not that
what was said could be rehearsed, or
the laughter or thunder taken back.
We wouldn't want it to be. We
wouldn't want it to be any
other way, in the end.

Amendments are offered to improve the plan,
but autumn slowly turns the light thin.
In the leaf's release the flash of green
still on the stem reminds us that
the glisten and the blossoms
come again. New verses of
seed to assist us yet.

HIS WONDER WAS OUR CLEAR MIDNIGHT

Any weakness you had, you weren't aware of.
Bravery and confidence filled your days.
Largeness supposed always. In reality, glowing.
In reality, knowing things only an old sage
might know, an ocean raging behind the eyes, dark flashes
and shadows of secrets stirring below. Head tipped,
gazing out farther, broader. Removing impediments meant
to bind, you revealed just enough clues for us to follow.

How could we learn the calm assuredness of mind it takes to
embrace more than our arm-throw? To resonate with
new ways of sounding, deeper than any before had traveled—
where breath was borrowed, where language swam up
from throats unknown, where the faces in the mirrored
waters were always familiar, the voices shared equally—
our chorus. What did your fullness teach us, if not to embrace—
passing strangers, your body, the shapes the tall grasses traced?

MY WAKING WAS MY WADING IN

The strength I didn't have, I sensed in fear
and lack of confidence. Smallness in buds
and leaf conceal the largeness of the later
blooms of summer, and though depression
nearly drowned me early, the impressions
left by time alone made me aware that
time alone could heal me. The soundness
of sleep, then, and the wildness and wideness
of dreams: the desert as the ocean floor,
whales swimming slowly in the pale blue
sky above me—dozens of them, in layers.
To stand before such enormity, to learn
the power of humility before the grander
risings could dawn within me, I curled
with the stories that left me full into being.
My head rocked back on my neck. I stared,
observed. Took note. Thrilled at the scope
and the potential, I held the same pose
as when I had stood, minutes before bedtime
on those crisp Mojave nights, and stared
at impossible blue stars scattered like spilled
sugar. I was a child. What did I know then
of the wild that shook me so deeply? What
new language did that emptiness teach me—
of words I didn't know I didn't know, awaiting
my arrival. I became fearless, walking up, stepping
in to that which threatened to silence me. I became
a swimmer alongside those leviathans of song.
I became the boat that would carry the weight in me,
the sail that brought the sounding breath along.

To Cytokinesis

PLAY TIME

the child
wet pats
to smooth
the mud
pie

tea party
mirth

she pours
the air
into
the cup
by

teddy bear
her

guest here
in her
garden
café
try

another
please

a kiss
for each
serving
now it's
bye

goodbye next
please

her lips
to mud
to taste
her goods
try

the cake and
tea

kiss the
ground to
thank her
friend the
earth

PRIMARY COLORS

Hands of the 4-color press operator
mirror her work: fresh ink flecks
on flesh with each pass—magenta,
cyan, yellow, and black. Specks

on her shoe tops, too, that her daughter
will reach for as she crawls to where she
sits, eyes closed, after work. As her daughter
will later reach for the confetti candy at her

third birthday party, trace every bright dot on each
Wonder Bread bought, laugh at the thought of her
once-favorite blouse, stare at the selvedge edge—
the row of circles aligned at the end of her comforter.

A LIFE

The morning rang to
life, as the young girl sang her
budding reflection.

The noon day sun ran
clear, as the woman wiped her
glasses and regrets.

The evening sky was
violet and gray, like her
hair in the mirror.

SOMNAMBULISM AND SLEEP

Displacing her water self, the woman filled with earth augments the musk of wet bark in pre-dawn. The trees respond by arranging the stars just for her, between branches, sweeping the sky to allow such re-framing of the past, ancient fires still sparking across vast distances, waves of warmth penetrating.

Emptied of sky, the woman filled with smoke listens to the night bird's lament, the rustle of leaves. Trusting nothing unseen, she navigates the circumstance of morning reluctantly, the necessary dew, the conductorless serenade of grasses and insects celebrating new arrangements of the universe all at once. She prefers the dark filters that separate the world from becoming too much. She prefers the silence of dusk, the more subtle leavenings and leavings in the misty spaces between rather than such bright fields, or the spikes of sun now amassed as glowing columns slanting through the canopy like pillars. What is supported by such beauty? Beauty itself? The volume of sparks manifest into creatures that animate the stillness for a brief time? To what end, she wonders.

And between the sheets of morning, the layers of light, between them both, the filtered memory of a lover's scent and the weavings of a common past, of hair and wind, of river grasses underwater echoing their dances. The tapestry of the sky stitched with birds and the migrations of threads across dark orbs, the spanning of opposites by the hidden ones who chant and sing in the colors of buried seeds.

THE WOMAN WHO PAINTS HEARTS ON STONES

She walks the deserts and meadows listening.
She hears the rocks and fallen feathers whisper to her.
Some stones she has found vibrate. They make her
fingers shake.
The birds and lizards listen with her.
Her dogs know this to be true.

She takes the stones home.
She paints hearts on the stones.
Some are larger, like in life.
She has seen bluish shadows cross the yellow sand,
and wept at that.
She has seen most of the things she loves
either fade or disappear.
Her heart has broken again and again.
She is not alone, even so.
She loves the mountain ranges looking over her.
She paints hearts.
It's easy for her. She can avoid thinking, and it makes her
feel better.
She finds balance in the doing.
Her dogs listen with her. The trees listen too.
Her heart knows this to be true.

She leaves the stones at nursing homes,
and hospitals, and cemeteries.
Those who find them feel better, too.
They come across them as she did.
First they frown at the heartstone, then they smile.
They flutter.
Sometimes their fingers shake.

Her heart sometimes feels better.
She worries about herself. About her mind.
She worries her heart is a stone now.
Her heart is not a stone.
The ones who love her know this to be true.

BECAUSE THE SKY WAS SOFT AND SLOW

upon waking, she found a smudged
shadow fading, found
it was not hard to turn to the light

and to rise and decide the anger
was no longer welcome
in her house. She forgave

the troubled sleeper behind her.
And so, the rest of her day
was a blouse of silk cascading
down smooth arms—

the rest of her life lit
from behind, a film she
would have enjoyed
seeing again after all.

SHOULD THEY ASK HER NAME

The one whose blood is the shadow
of a dance of strangers, who has known
mostly loss, whose hair dissolves now
into the white of the security lamp
high on the wall above her head,
near neighborhoods of families whose
children are taught to fear her and
those who look like her—she knows
that she is more shadow than name.

She asks for change. Then a cigarette.
The man walking past offers instead
a shake of his head, quickly, without
looking over, on his way to that liquor
store's front door. In four hours he will
be drunk. She will still be here, asking
the same questions, her spine leaning
on the sharp corner of the building's
edge, the pain a new brightening
within her—one wing of wall in light
and leading to glass and the sound of
human voices, the other wall falling
away behind her to more dissolving.

HALF OF THE WORLD IS ALWAYS IN DARKNESS

Awakening, the woman finds
her ear slightly suctioned to
the pavement beneath her—
pain that had manifested in
her dream as a hot towel being
pressed to her face while she
sat crying, taking a bite from
a badly bruised apple—while in
a hospital? She can't recall. She
sits up now. Rubs her cheek.
And ear. And neck. Half of her
is red.

On the other side of the earth—
now night—directly where her ear
had been pointed while she slept,
men dressed in black and white had been signing
papers, raising glasses,
toasting to agreements that
would eventually lead to events that would cause
more nightmares, that would see her and her
family suffer even more. She had not heard
those glasses clinking, of course.
Too much world between them.

THE WOMAN CRUSHED BY THE SCHOOL NOW RUBBLE

She is thirsty. Why hasn't anyone heard her asking for water?
Her child is no longer at her side. She must be thirsty too.

She screams for water again. For her daughter first.
But she has not been screaming. Only in her dream.

Now a wave of calm at last. She is coming to understand.
Someone has been placing gemstones on her naked body.

She sobs once, relieved that her child's thirst was not real.
She becomes lighter—is lifted—liberated that she is not ashamed

at her flesh upturned and open to the sky, offered now freely
to whatever jeweler it is that is adorning her so lovingly.

The saffron sun reflects off silver tongs hovering over her,
holding a banded agate that gets placed gently at her throat.

Turquoise ovals are set on each toe of her left foot.
A gold chain laid to trace the center of her forearm,

crossing her wrist, trailing off her finger
like a running faucet. A trickle, warm.

An emerald is placed on her
forehead as a third eye

by the loving one in white
who cares for her.

But the thirst returns,
awakens a pulsing pain,

and the one dressing her
turns into a surgeon,

with scalpel, attending
to her jeweled body.

But no.
She is on dirt.

Pinned down.
And now the terrible weight.

Her eyelids flutter
as if wings awakening

as she recalls the whistle
of drone missile approaching

and the shrieking scream
overhead just before it hit.

Now she remembers.
She had been praying.

Her child lifted as the ground rebounded.
An angel messenger? No—

She opens her eyes at the horror of it.
Her girl flying up and away.

A cloud of dust and flame.
Then she knows.

She is not being dressed,
or operated on, or attended to.

She is dying,
and her clothes are burning off of her.

The emerald is an ember
of wood debris smoldering.

The gold chain melds into
a gully sliced down her arm.

The agate becomes a hole in her.
The turquoise, her missing toes.

The lapis lazuli, blue shrapnel
that has turned her spine to river.

The generals, adorned with shining medals in a room
far away, are congratulated for their surgical precision.

END-OF-THE-MONTH RITUAL

The crying child's chin wobbled
dragging the flow of morning back
like the bad wheel on the shopping cart—
and both helped sustain the annoyance
of the mother there, pushing, struggling
to cope with not enough in her purse
to pay for all she needed that day,
and with no hope of earning more cash
any time soon. Knowing this, yet still
filling the cart with everything on the list
anyway—a kind of acting that allowed
them to live in a different world, if only
for a moment, where it all was okay—
like the made up phone conversations
of her child, half-gibberish, and with
no one on the other end. At the checkout,
then, the end of the play: the painful
dénouement, unloading of items back
off the belt and out of bags already full.
More shaking (and in her now as well)
plus a browful pout that would last
the entire bus ride home, despite her
hand patting the leg: *There, there. I know.*

OVERTIME

The woman rolling the ceiling with paint
holds the pole like a broomstick, as if she's
sweeping the floor of some inverted world.
At first a splotch on her forearm appears.
Then across the bridge of her nose, a plop
on her shoe, in her hair, everywhere. Were
she to paint all day she would disappear.
Blend completely into the room. Become
her work. Her neck will carry the stiffness
for days, even so. She will find relief
only by looking down, chin to chest, the
best of her labors above her ignored.

CHARITY

On the north side of her shelter,
    moss.

On the other side of worth,
    his loss.

For the taking pride will shove
    away.

For the giving Earth, another
    day.

GARDENING AS SELF-HELP

Her resolve then untangled.
Complications would be met
without hesitation. She led
the loose ends through eyelets,

laced up, and braced herself
for the cold. What got shelved

would store without regrets.
She carried only what fed
her hourly needs, and set
to pull weeds that strangled.

WAITING FOR THE MUSIC TO RESUME

The fruit disregarded
shrinks and hardens.

She was trying to tell him
she didn't know.

He tried to imagine her walk then,
straight and certain.

How the walls softened
when the news came.

How they tried to speak
of a future without knowing.

How things became more precious
after, the tenderness more apparent.

§

Outside, an egg wobbling
in a nest flecked with shells.

A string that once marked the place
of celebration still knotted to the railing.

Inside, worry displacing
sleep in bed.

The broken violin, mute, yet still holding
the room for the light tracing its curves.

The hard tragedy of neglect
while repair can still be done.

The maestro looks up expectantly,
the tempo already moving in his head.

EATING A PLUM IN THE DARK

She imagines what remains before
her now, before she continues, before
the rest has been ingested. Based on
the taste in her mouth, her future
with him can now be imagined.
Based on the degree of hunger
sated, she gauges the worth of
the swallows remaining, of her
need to even continue—the feeling
of emptiness in the fullness felt
(or half-fullness). She considers
putting that half-eaten fruit down,
unfinished, and selecting instead
another from the large glass bowl
sitting now at the center of her
table. She could easily reach over
and place her hand on another,
and it would fit her grip as if it
were destined for her (but she
knows better). Instead, she slows
her chewing and pauses, the half-
plum suspended in front of her
chin, her hand rocked back from
the wrist, weighing the stone
and the flesh. She closes her eyes
(even though the darkness engulfs
her completely now) and wishes for
more, imagines the orchard outside
and how it looked just after
the last downpour as she walked
down the rows alone, each tree

dark with soaked bark, the rich
smells of the mud and breezes,
and thousands of plums dripping—
each one a sun hung, glistening
before her, and just for her if she
wanted it. She sits, swallows hard,
her hand still poised, her mouth
like a blossom, curious in the darkness.

X

> After "Sonnet X," from "Sonnets from an Ungrafted Tree" by Edna St. Vincent Millay

Outside of the rattling window, an ungrafted tree, still bearing cross-hatch notch marks where he had planned to add branches of a similar species, to expand the garden in color and bloom, scent and harvest. Too many seasons ago to remember exactly. He had been more ambitious than capable, she discovered, and the room inside now holds two versions of his failures. Soon to be one—not by agreement but by death decided. She still cares for him, on levels that have changed over time, and so she has returned as caregiver.

But not for him. To care for his mother, as he can not. She is there for him after all, then. And what would the neighbors say if they knew: the ex-wife returning to their old home together? Scandalous, it might have appeared from the outside—or would have decades ago, not knowing how the hard winters of chill had brought both vernalization and permission from the other to bloom elsewhere. And how resentment loses its color over time to finally run clear and cleanse and bond with things once our enemy.

She views their marriage now the way an adult gazes on a scar from childhood: Detached. And with the kiss of pain long past, it stands for something other than the place of an old wound healed. The accident once so all-consuming had emptied fast, grown over with proud flesh much shinier than the duller uninjured surroundings. Replacement a part of the punctuation of the body—an em-dash in her life's narrative once connecting a second sentence, become scar as minus sign. Nothing left to take away. Divorce had changed her.

Far more than he had. And it was, in the end, for the better. And for his mother, too, now residing in their old home—whose every exhale now brings a rattle as she dreams of round Meyer lemons hung bright against smaller limes on the tree outside, the one her son had grafted. The dream is warm, and once it fades she will cough, drawing the look of her former daughter-in-law, who will stroke her arm, trace Xs across purple splotches, sing softly to her. Each act there now proof that this is a time of grace, a house of love.

TO SYNTHESIS

WHAT DOESN'T FIND THE CENTER FINDS THE SHADOW

push of try
and not of win

pull of search
but over found

play amass
full laughter blend

still we hold
the gazes still

edges lose sharp
to the darkness

tune of grey
less more but no

surrender of
retreat of light this

souvenir this blaze
still in us

THE SAMENESS CHANGING

We are never the same.
You and I and every other
are different, and that will always
be. And every different one of us, we
are always changing, always changing
form. Literally. Cells sloughing. A constant
conversion of mass. Sunlight providing
all of the energy, all transformed
into chemistry and rearranged.
A steady exchange. Daylight
gets absorbed and converted
into orange, or apple, or
pear. We eat sunshine.
We are star stuff.

We are always the same.
You and I and everyone, no
different, and that will always
be. And all is spent on each other:
we are always paying it back, always
exchanging all of us back to the source
with cells revising atoms in constant
conversion of the same matter that
provides all of the building blocks.
Atomic forms in chemical trees,
rearranging. Every body the
same—the blurring takes
form and we shine
(with) the source.
And that is
enough.

THE WAX BUDDHA MELTS INTO SLUMBER

The candle reforms to the saucer beneath it.
The couch edge hangs loose where the puppy has chewed.
The alphabet soup overboils into commas.
The hangers form asterisks in the big box.

The broken clock's hour hand points to the heavens.
The salvaged nails rust in the can on the shelf.
The junk drawer corks roll with the pull of those searching.
The batteries leak in the flashlight's curved dark.

The sea water drips from the cracked plastic bucket.
The blue shovel falls in the hole it has dug.
The wedding ring hides on the ocean's soft bottom.
The handprints in sand castles fade with the dusk.

The tissue piñata turns pulp in the gutter.
The ribbon is twisted around the chair leg.
The party balloon dulls and softens to wrinkles.
The punch stains red stars on the tablecloth lace.

The old rug is rolled up in weeds on side yard.
The rut in the mud holds the bike tire in place.
The sundial rusts as it sits in the shadows.
The garden hose signature changes each day.

[...MORE AT CHANCE]

Cadenza cries
in earthquakes:
cadence rests,

operatic gaps.
We hold our
breath, ourselves,

each other—try
a modicum of laughter
at shaking credenzas

and breaking plates:
bones to culm.
(...more to come)

WHAT THEN IS SEEN

Between what we hope and what becomes,
an ocean.

Between what we intend and what is heard,
a sky.

If a grid of consequence could be placed
—somehow, laid over—

the chaos of our random acts,
what then?

We might draw a map of our misintentions.
We might see what's not learned from neglect.

Between the imagined plans
and the grasses that rise,

long breaths
that turn to longer sighs.

Between the dream of home
and the place we reside,

a river that turns
and turns.

If a circle encompassing all we have changed
were overlaid beyond our lives

—how A caused B and B begat C—

we might see there is no end to it.

A greater web become apparent.
But what then?

We might weave a story of change,
and thereby change ourselves.

What becomes an ocean: our hope.
What is heard: a sky intended.

UNFORESEEN CONSEQUENCES

The jagged line
of the crack in the pot,
once repaired, became
the strongest spot.

The hungry one
got hungrier, but
by knowing that pain,
became more giving.

Where the bag was torn
the seeds escaped. Now
flowers line the path
where the poor man walked.

ONCE HE THOUGHT HE CHANGED

    What he
            once
                  thought
  of the fields
                    he walked
                          changed
            once
                  he walked
  beyond
    the fields

    What he
            once
                  thought
  of his leaving
                          changed
            once
                  he left

            once
                  he left
  it to the
                          changes
                  he
                          changed

FOR NOW

The quiet yet powerful
voices in our lives.

The small but precious
things of this world.

The slant of light
across the table,

where we sit
and say nothing.

Content in just
this moment,

our time together
enough.

There when you need them.
Here as a reminder,

across our hands
Content in this.

This—

The quiet yet powerful
voices in our lives.
There when you need them.
The small but precious
things of this world.

Here as a reminder.
The slant of light
across the table,
across our hands,
where we sit
and say nothing.
Content in this.
Content in just
this moment.
This—
our time together
enough.

OF FLIGHT AND COMMUNION

burble of cumulus
around aluminum
        shine lifts my love
        with thirty rows of others
in a theater hurled across
high and over

some of us stumble
from wanderlust leaving
        those we love pining
        behind and below still
reunions lift and we share
the sum of loss undercover

accumulated stubble
surprising as we fumble
        to re-sync clocks and shave
        lag and locks but for now
we shuffle through what
terminal hours uncover

LEVELS OF SMELL

Highest up, outer space (which space suits returned from space walks confirm) smells like an arc welder's shop—images of a blue collar god with orange sparks flying, and a workbench of worn tools, spare parts, sweat and safety goggles (where the metaphor breaks down).

Clouds smell like rivers, with traces of ocean and earth—cloud connoisseurs, like pilots who fly with open cockpits, might offer cloud reviews like fine wines: "A bright cumulus with traces of oak-leaf dew, abundant fruit and a hint of finishing cirrus charcoal..." (though blind smell tests might find them all full of baloney).

Prop plane engines trail only oily scents.

The smell of goose wing bears traces of swamp.

Skyscrapers ooze a hint of wet concrete and steel from bolts (and the finer noses will detect the ammonia from glass cleaner residue after the first rain of the season).

Redwoods smell of rain, which smells like clouds (see above)—though their needles will drop and acquire the must and musk of the forest floor, like a damp dish rag left in a stack of bowls in the sink for too long.

Some old roofs smell of tar in the bright sunshine, but old barns smell of moss and lumber when it rains.

In the farmhouse kitchen, the tin lunch pail smells of baloney, the silver thermos sharp with coffee.

On the floor, the dog food bowl smells of horses, and the panting breath of the sleeping dog beside smells much like the rest of the farm.

LEVELS OF NOISE

Highest up, the edge of space crackles in blue-black for no ears to hear. Cloud mist whispers are dampened in the softness of others clouds. Jet turbines carve cylinders of spiraling shrieks across the pale sky, drifting down to become just a wind-broken hum by the time they reach the housewife in the yard, her ears covered by a cyan scarf as she fastens lemon-yellow clothespins onto damp white sheet hems.

The drone of a solo Cessna plane over rural farms causes cows to stop chewing and stand like groups of statues as they listen—before chewing, mooing, and looking back down. Inner-city pigeons whistle with wing flaps, coo-purr to each other on sky-scraper ledges, then bustle and mumble about traffic and lunch trash from the dirty sidewalks. Power lines buzz in silver slices across black highways. Palm tree fronds rustle in noontime breezes.

Sheets and pillow cases snap in the gusts of late afternoon, a taut rope clothesline twanging, one cyan scarf hung as a comma between the loads. Hedge trimmers cut green boxes to eye level. Push mowers chop in roulette-wheel rhythms. Obligate anaerobes replicate in sighs on mucous membrane's microflorae. Sweat drops to the grass in dull thumps, muffled explosions on the ladybug's black and red.

The rotting roots of the dead tree hum with ants. The soil below moans with worms. Stones deep under the ground tick and clack as they settle with the seasons. Bones wait in the quiet dark after all of the clicking and cracking. The rest is silence.

LEVELS OF SIGHT

Highest up (farthest out / away), Voyager 1 voyages through interstellar space (the cold, cold regions between the stars), gazing with ones and zeroes to points of light shining (or reflecting) in the far, far dark beyond our planetary system—and what does she level her sights on now? Chaotic stars and groups of stars and galaxy swirls and groups of swirls and all beautiful in their pullings on one other (for now—in eight years she will grow blind from old age, at just 48).

Next up / out / away is Voyager 2, a slight misnomer (or anachronistic moniker?) as she was birthed first from the Earth, but turned her gaze instead to the larger planets along the way, and took her time tracing a line straight through Saturn's rings—and now she awaits the same fate as she chases behind her younger, faster twin (though she'll never catch her)—these two blind sisters, our most distant relatives.

A few rovers on Mars, also blind, or soon to be, roll on.

Hundred of probes and satellites and artificial eyes across the solar system, each sending radio signal 1-0 neurons back to the brains here at earth to decode.

On the Earth's Moon, more than 400 tons of man-made junk is strewn, mostly eyeless, but some gazing at the horizon and noting each Earthrise with flat stares.

A shell of satellites (and space debris) hugs the Earth, most just relay stations, but looking back down (closer / in) to specific concave dishes—matching eyes tipped their way to catch their gaze, pulling.

And here on Earth, everywhere, billions of eyes drawing their beads and focusing, each with direct lines of sight to ancient suns they'll never reach (though blind sister chase each other here as well, their heads tipped back, their gazes the farthest reaching of all).

To Organisms

FEMME FATALE AS APPLIED TO FOOD

The fish will be most remembered
as its corpse upon the plate,
or recalled through the years
as the Valentine's Day dinner
he made, despite its entire
life of swimming in the sea.

The fowl get photographed
dead as well, on a skewer
over fire—but suspended in
the air, at least (a more fitting
end for a bird). And it will fly

once again, but as a series of zeroes
and ones in code when that pic
gets sent from a smart phone,
then uncoded and uploaded
to become a post on Instagram—
not as a chicken, but as shish kabob.

The steer is not remembered
for its dusty days on the ranch,
nor the pig in the sty, nor the egg
in the coop—yet all are recalled as
the Breakfast Special, and whatever's
leftover, just soup.

COINCIDENCES

Somewhere in the world are two people—
one on a lunch break, one at breakfast—
each bringing a crisp apple to their lips
at the exact same instant. The soundtrack
of the one would match the other's exact
for that one brief act if it were switched.

Somewhere there are two other strangers
who speak the same words simultaneously:
"I'm sorry" (though one stares blankly
and the other frowns and looks away).

Today a woman in South Sudan
and a man in Quảng Ngãi, Vietnam,
each patted their hungry infant
at the same moment, and sighed.

You and I, when were both just babies, might
have shared the same observation (of two dogs
who just met, maybe, and looked at each other
then yawned as one), and we, perhaps, each
smiled then and pointed the same, as if
choreographed—the way we just now laughed
in tandem today, and called the other's name.

THE WEAKNESS WE TAKE FROM OURSELVES

Slowly we straighten
after the shoe falls. From
motion to stillness. Bare-
foot, then naked. It is late.

The flash of our skin in
the mirror seems birdlike
in the half-dark. Nature
is simple: a straight line

sets the horizon—level.
From there, complexity
arises; then more bending
and variation the higher one

goes. Then things fall in
a straight line, perpendicular,
once it's over. When the wren
swoops into her nest, the curve

meets itself in a circle.
The room darkens. We undress.
Our faces seem to whorl and blend
in the glass the more we stare.

But we do. We can't look away.
We can't end this embrace, even
when the end is near. Even when
it takes our breath away. We can't.

THE NIGHT THAT UNITES US

What else is joined, then, when one by one we
weave our nights and gather our far cities
together? Perhaps what the shiver of
the petals whispered to the thorns, and how
the flower was stronger for it. What we
bring to each other each time we simply
sit and share those silences that tell all
we want to say but can't. Not enough time.
The landscapes of your laughter, the shadows
your body leaves on the walls as the first
lamps of evening come on, the way I will
trace that with my eyes after you have gone.
The hours pardon us in their giving,
and still we remain prisoners of days
spent apart. And still we hold on to those
things we cannot see yet somehow know: sun
on the window warming the room where the
other one sleeps late. The ache of doubt. What
the river tells the mountain as it lifts
it in small ways and carries it closer
to the ocean. How pain both wastes and saves
us, and the pressure of storms. The taste of
your mouth: what the rain does to the desert.

NOT TIRED

You will throw out your arms
to unlikely skies. I will try
not to act surprised by the ease, by
the slope of your smile, by alarms

sounding in the flowers only now awakening
(pistil clappers quaking). You shall keep
your steps long, spanning rocks, steep
shadows of yucca and juniper ringing.

What the bells trace across tall grass is what
    I hope to bring (but subtler).
    Should things break while I'm away
(or lost inside a hard thought that sinks
    my softness) would you mind, as such?
Or will you laugh, despite, exhausted?
    Would you think me a puzzle of too much
trouble? Or, will you swing my stubborn gate,
    kick away the stone's dark mosses to say:

"I shall sing of your large givings always"
    (as I do for you). And
you for me, just now, as night-sparks
    implicate your smile, your swimming hands.

BURNING CROPS

> "You cannot feel the heat unless
> you put your hands in the coal."
> —Anonymous proverb

Your gaze at the burning field holds,
despite the smoke. Distant hems

of flame link ash to green, lift
heat that flutters trees to azure

and births a cloud of silent birds.
The day's final breezes curl

dusky haze across the landscape.
This ache, purveyor of nothing,

takes my strength, would take my life
if I let it. But I love that

memory far too much to let
it go, even if you've left

ahead of me. So, I endure
the smoldering nocturnes, let grief

release itself into thickening night—
lost moths tumbling away from light.

COMFORT FOR THE ONE WHO WAITS IN PATIENCE

The warming after the downpour
is what I wanted to remind you of.
What I wish I could show you now:
powdered coat of the berry shed
(temporarily) with the dew, how
the flood that displaces can also
erase the dullness accrued. Know
that in the darkness as you slept
(I might offer) the pre-dawn sky left
a sheen on the walk, small beads on
everything even slightly horizontal.
And how in that still and soft weeping
in your dream, at that same moment
you lie shaking, unaware, clear globes
were forming beyond your worry.
Even as you slept on then, the awakening
of birds sensing the sun about to emerge,
and wings, unseen, lifting scents to calm.
In the windless grove you had walked
before, whose fruit-heavy branches once
scratched the sky with blossoms (the strange
longhand from childhood days and old
unfinished stories), there comes a new
stirring: a reminder of second chances.
Lost harvests (or what you thought to be
lost) appear anew, reach through somehow.
A berry stitching a liquid sky, dropping
at the same pace as the rain surrounding,
lands softly on soft ground, unharmed.
Maybe this will be what is noticed most,
not the loudest boast or hurtful lie

(from the one now behind you that
you once so trusted), but the barely said
(under the breath) clear and noble truth.
The clarity that comes with morning
chores, those small rewards—a white bowl
of fresh fruit reflected beneath itself on
the polished table, bright and dusted.

NIGHTHAWKS AND DAWN CHORUS

Slaked and sated, we balanced on the last
leg of the night: hoisted one final glass
and settled in with whispers.
                        I dreamed of
whistling feathers overhead in the
darkness. You kicked a limb as in your dream
the bird perched strangely sideways looked down the
branch as if a long bar glowing, leading
into a new song.
                    In morning's slow slide
across the bed, we decided, laughing
and rolling, that the first leg out and off
the edge, the bold maker of coffee and
slicer of melon, would be the one to
have their say for the rest of the day.

ALL-ENCOMPASSING

> After Lu Ji's *Wên Fu*, fourth century A.D.,
> and "Cinder" by Susan Stewart, 2017

The bottle,
which is glass
blown by breath
in fire, then
cooled by water,
is later used to
carry more water
to the fire to
cool another bottle
which has been
blown by breath.

The axe blade,
forged in fire
and pounded
by other steel
swung, itself
becomes swung
against the wood
of tree, the man
swinging it
panting hot air,
cooled by water
from a bottle
blown by breath
in fire and cooled
by water.

The tree
is felled
by an axe,
then halved
by a blade,
the halves sawn
into logs, then
logs into lumber,
which is then
shaped by
a large axe into
a smaller version
of itself until
that hatchet
is paired
with blade
and hung
beside the one
who shaped it
into its own image.

The tree sprouts suckers
that are smaller versions
of itself, and which will
grow themselves into
full trees which look like
the eldest one, and which
will eventually sprout other
suckers in their own shade
to make more, and more again.

The water, which has followed the shape
of the tree it rained against, likewise embraces

the forms of both the larger axe and the smaller
hatchet, generation after generation of iterations
running toward the source, being lifted back up,
defining in each moment one part of another
thing touched along the way, by way of that
touching—simultaneously finding those shapes
that define our own shape through this life,
which is reiterated and shared. Into the ground
or down with the waterfalls and rivers, the water
seeks its level, absorbed in soil or tapped by tree,
evaporated or re-purposed, or flowing freely
all the way to the sea, back to the larger source—
that blue bottle it once help define which is
now defining its shape anew as it fills it again.

POURING WATER FROM A LARGER VESSEL INTO A SMALLER VESSEL

The water becomes like the sky, taking the shape of what it fills.
The sky, once displaced, surrounds instead. It is indiscriminate
in its embrace—caresses without possessing, sympathetic
to the shapes of things it is not (as we are, when at our best).

And in turn, the breeze will become the sky's new pouring,
increasing its understanding of all that cannot contain,
engulfing that which it will become, in carbon fixation—
flowers and pistils now shaken awake, now still again.

My father's form has found itself anew in me.
When I was a child, his father pointed to the Milky Way
and shook his head, tears welling. In time,
the water seeks the sky's slow relief in ascension.

We will relive these days of desert heat in the hours before
sleep finally comes, so much sky above our heads.

BESTOWAL

If someday someone tries to imagine
what we were like,

  tell them to look at the symmetry
  of red rocks layering the mountains.

If someone asks
if things were hard,

  point to the shadows
  the moonlight throws on the garden.

If anyone ponders
what we brought to each other,

  tell them to look to the skies
  as they open above the ocean.

If anyone is curious
if our lives moved smoothly,

  refer them to the electrons orbiting freely,
  reordering in accordance with the forces that be.

If you ever wonder
how I felt,

  turn to the leaves
  that turn and return.

ALL, ALL ALIKE

The dirt on my dog's paws
smells of what I love:
Earth exposed.
Proof of being in it,
of walking through it—
raw, connected,
endeared,
unleashed.

Lichen
sheds sea
as tides withdraw.
The dock sings hours
of wakes, creaks through the night.
Worth endures
with love. Small things of
the world teach largeness.

FALLINGS-OUT WHILE DRESSING

Our cat poses and shows us her profile.
I'll pet her to get her to purr. My dog
supposes he knows what is best with his
nose nudges pressing against us both.
We'll converse about their importance
in this universe, each one insisting that
they are the far superior one. I refuse to
choose, knowing I'll not hear the end of it,
either way—knowing their fur will address
more arguments across all I wear today.

THEN I WILL ROLL AGAIN WITH THEM

When my life force,
fading, forces
the issue—

the issue
of my parents:
their light

combined,
manifest
as this, my form—

when that spark
pulsing the heart
in me runs its energies

to dim,
to dimmer,
to darkness—

then perhaps it will be
that all of what I have
ever thought or done,

all of the awkward
and graceful
animations of this flesh,

will simply vanish—
vanish as did all
of the love I had missed

or denied
in my ignorance
and selfishness.

Or, perhaps it will be
that all of that light
generated through

all of the love I have
ever given, forgiven,
been given

will shine once again,
manifest back
into some memory

of worldly flesh
aglow. If so,
may it appear

then before me
in the form of
my old dogs—

all of them—
all bounding up
to meet me

after all
this time apart,
and then lead me

once again
(as they did before)
out of the darkness.

PART II:
FROM THE HORIZON

To the Ocean's Daughter

BEFORE THE POET WENT TO BED

In case the perfect line should arrive
while he was turned away, he set a net
below the mailbox to catch any letter
or word or note delivered by nightbird

feather falling, or woven by red spider
in the ledgers of the mesh. An imperfect
circle drawn around his house with cinder
saved from yesterday's fire. A potion

of white candle wax and black ash of wick
mashed with pestle of thighbone and pressed
into the frozen hinges of a box kept hidden
under the floorboards, in hopes the paste

might loosen. He worked the syntax
of his folding bones to sit cross-legged
in the grass, then he lay himself back at last
to watch the suns circle around Polaris,

the universe beyond rising in slow motion
over his fence, one blue point of light at a time.
He held out his thumb and closed one eye.
He ached for the rest. But he knew, at last:

such rituals of resolve and alignment with
any partial truth glimpsed, the smaller arcs
of his orbit were futile in the greater mystery—
save for the small relief pressed into the grass,

the depression of the page, the ruts made
in the plane of his brief passing. But for now,
the resolution of night, and all dissolving
anew into the blank fields of the morning.

IN PRAISE OF SLOW AND SILENT GROWTH

To close the gap where longing reigns as king
the morning will send you a wordless song
that emerges at dawn from her slender
throat, pure as a river's warble over
smooth stones, sung openly as a bird trills
without score or predetermined structure,
without worrying where there may be ears
or an empathetic heart in the world
to witness such bright unfolding. She is
that moment when "known" and "seeking" blend to
a moving crescendo. The tip of throat
that is perfect—just enough for the fine
balance of light and niche of story that
the flesh holds. Enough to save us. Enough
to share. I will deliver it to you
in my own voice, if you wish—though know it's
a poor imitation. Still, such songs of
praise should be sung, and unashamedly.
A lingering will remain, too, beyond
the song itself. Just enough. Just enough,
we find this world. Barely in time, but we
find it. This truth and more I wish for you:
success achieved in perfect grace; a hand-
hold to secure; depth of gaze to bridge the
days lost between us; and the songbird's full
crescendo—fulfillment of the promise
I brought to you this daybreak with a bowl
of fruit and cream and the paper, like me,
still warm and folded, awaiting your hands.

I HEARD SOMETHING SINGING

From another room,
someone doing the laundry.
A worker outside walking home,
hands throbbing and warm,
has made the evening lighter.
How to find that singing place?

When I first felt the hum
vibrate my skin to tingle, I knew
I must let it in, let it soar through me.
To open up rooms inside of me
sealed away for so long, only to find
the song already there.

Whether you brought it, a gift
left behind, or if it was always inside,
something came alive in the breathing,
formed a lilt until all I knew intoned
with light, a shared vibration I
could attend to, a ringing grace.

MUSE GAZE

En pointe, her focus fixed
on me (or not), she seems
to be looking through me
to infinity. With each new
revolution I catch her eyes,
glimpse something somehow
through them. A deep ache,
then, to offer something
of worth in return, exist
as a counter-anchor that
I might assist her in keeping
her center, keeping her
here. I would step out of
my flesh to join her, flood
rooms of childhood by
breaching levees and tanks,
set fire to yellowed edges
of manuscripts coded
and curled within me,
unscrew hinges, crowbar
locks and pry away jambs,
knock down fire blocks
and drywall sheets that
hold back sleep narratives
swelling as tides toward
the moon that shimmers
across the water's surface
which she rides as she turns
and turns—slow pirouettes
of gratitude for a voice to
her own mute mouthings,

an open kiss to blow from
her spinning, like the earth
emerging from her curve
of shadow across the pages,
reminder of another light
hiding, that I might now
swallow and turn to song.

WATERMARK ANGELS

    After "The Angel Is My Watermark"
    by Henry Miller

Better half an angel than none.
A silhouette of clarity left on a dusty car hood.
Any evidence will suffice when it comes
to proof of presence.

To be authentic in ink, that is concern number one.
To simply go on writing more and more.
To commit to making marks, emitting ghosts,
getting nearer to release.

Freeing, to paint without concern
of better or best. To lean right or left
and stay in the boat. To be willing to capsize,
to fall in then,

to watch with flooded eyes the pigment
lift off your hands, your skin.
To dissolve completely in that sinking or rising.
Such joy is free to give. Is freely given.

I MUST SING

Now that my mind has memorized
the salt-worn lines of your blood tides
the rhythms of your breath against my chest
(I have found a way for that to live in me
even when you are not here in the flesh)
the way black notes and clefs in silence
are used to lift a melody within, the way
brass horns boom in patches of color
the silence that sings blooms of blue-green patina
(now that my mind has learned the score)
I can listen

Now that I know
the rivers on the back of the hand
all return to you, my heart
I must sing

Now that I am singing your name
now that I am
now that
now

is something

AFTER LIGHT

That the moon rose soft
and fell dim in the day,
a pale watermark on paper,
a dime lost on the silver
bottom of the fountain,
and that I chased it anyway.

That I have lost nights
calling the ocean's daughter
to bless these pages, to send
a whisper from the breakers,
but heard only my own breath
rising, and swam out anyway.

That the waters carried me there
upon the rolling backs of waves.
That the spray hissed half a word,
which I sang back whole to a sky
that held both the sun and moon.
That I looked, and did not look away.

PART III:

FROM A SERIES
OF MARKING STONES:
APHORISMS, ANALOGIES,
AND OBSERVATIONS

To

FROM A SERIES OF MARKING STONES: TO

§

To misplace something
is to discover the price of neglect.

To say the empty tablet is hungry
is to think of the book as thirsty for attention.

To lose the map is to gain adventure.

To forget the plan is to find freedom.

To leave a book out in the rain
is to both change the story
and show the book's thirst.

When You

FROM A SERIES OF MARKING STONES: WHEN YOU

§ 1 §

When you get mad at inanimate objects,
you are doing it wrong.

When you are a newborn,
everything is very strange indeed.

When you retrace your steps after losing your keys, you
become an actor, playing yourself—back when you were less
aware. Or dumber.

When you are a three-year-old,
a nickel is worth more than a dime.
Because it's bigger.

When you are six, it makes no sense
why every day can't be your birthday.

When you are a maid hired to clean a dirty house, your
work will be noticed more than usual, even if you do a half-
assed job.

When you are a lover of diversity and newness, the world is
ever beautiful.

When you are an addict, what matters most is the next high.

When you are on the last leg of your journey home, the road
goes on like a cliché: forever.

When you worry, you waste.

When you tuck your legs far under so you can swing again
on the old swing set of your youth, you are doing it right.

§ 2 §

When you say "mama,"
it resembles the sounds
she made when she first held you.

When you sneeze,
the contraction and release reset you.

When you regret,
you re-weep.

When you feel nostalgia
(*nóstos* "a return home" + *álgos* "pain, suffering"), it is
nothing like the feeling of returning home after a grand
slam.

When you are grateful,
you are humble.

When you call a cat to come,
you are an optimist.

When you give a dog a treat,
the gift is equally yours.

When you dream about apple picking
after a frosty day of climbing ladders and picking apples,
your two feet ache
in two realms at once.

When you see someone smile who is broken-hearted,
unseen are the knots and the secret weavings that hold
things in place from the other side, like the threads on the
back of a tapestry, crossing, stretched.

When you tap your fingers,
you type gibberish.

When you sweat,
you seep.

When you weep with another,
you absorb.

When you soak in a steaming jacuzzi,
you both absorb and release, as when you partake in a
good conversation.

When you sunbathe at the beach,
you bask in a radiation that can give life
or kill it, depending.

When you enjoy the smell of new mown grass, you take
pleasure in the chemistry of distress, released by the blades
to warn sister grasses of the crisis in progress.

When you give someone a rose in a vase,
you offer a dismembered, dying thing as a symbol of your
love.

When you rush to judgment,
you are often wrong.

When you analyze well before deciding,

you are often wrong, as well.

When you shave,
you save face.

When you say "mom,"
you hum twice.

§ 3 §

When you nudge,
your elbow becomes a tongue.

When you hold a grudge,
you hold a blank list that will never be filled.

When you wish ill on someone,
you hold the poison within.

When you are lazy,
you disrespect the gift of the sunshine.

When you are sorrowful,
you are too much in the past.

When you embrace someone, your heart becomes a mirror, thumping in syncopation, inches away, inches away.

When We

FROM A SERIES OF MARKING STONES: WHEN WE

§ 1 §

When we embrace, we forget long distances.

When we grow distant, we forget we leave a long wake of coldness.

When we grow cold, we fall asleep to grace.

When we lose grace, we shrink inside a bit— until a shaking insists that we awaken.

When we awaken, we remember to embrace.

§ 2 §

When we sing of what's right, what's wrong is implied.

When we tune to the ocean, our song is the tide.

You Are

FROM A SERIES OF MARKING STONES: YOU ARE

§ 1 §

You are "homeful" if you see
everywhere as your home,
regardless of any deed
or key you own
(or don't).

You are "poemful" if you listen
to the whispers of the garden,
regardless of the yard, or
weeds, or whether you
will see the seeds
sprout in time
(or won't).

You are a "grown up" when you
own up and take the blame
without excuses,
and apologize
for mistakes
you made.

You are "shown up" when you
think you have it sewn up
and so, phone it in—
but you lose it
when another
tries harder
and takes
it away.

§ 2 §

You are not apart,
no matter how
much you
try to be,
or think
you are.

You are set apart
by your particular
particles—the atomic
arrangement
of star ash
you are.

You are
like everyone
one and the same,
nevertheless. Yes,
never the less
you are.

What

FROM A SERIES OF MARKING STONES: WHAT

§ 1 §

What we don't see of love the first time we're in it is often what causes that first love to fail.

What we learn from love after it leaves us (or we leave it) is what we'll lean on instead of love the next time.

What love leaves us with lasts longer than the love.

§ 2 §

What we first see when we first fall in love is the radiance of time dissolving to nothingness.

What we first feel is bliss meeting bliss.

What we feel with the first kiss feels like a promise, like tomorrow is reaching back to save us.

What we first think taints whatever follows, skews our awareness and fairness of judgment.

What will be remembered of the last time we see that first love will be the radiance of the last kiss, tinged now with sorrow.

What lasts is sometimes the last thing thought, but more often than not, what lasts is the last thing we would have thought.

As

FROM A SERIES OF MARKING STONES: AS

§ 1 §

As the dew collects on the edge of a petal,
the blade of the shovel, blades in the meadow,
so shall you emerge, dripping wet again
into the world.

As the sky slowly lightens near the horizon, as pinpoint stars
fade like stones dropped in water, so shall you be displaced
by such turnings, so shall you rise to greet the day.

As the spider spins a new line from center, swings itself out
to find more through darkness, so shall you work through
this night without fearing, so shall you compose yourself.

As the sundial's face will grow warm with morning, as its
shadow follows continual purpose, so shall you be so moved.

As the fabric that became my shirt
will become my form, draping my shape,
taking on the same volume that I have displaced from the
sky, so my acts that hang beyond my presence will define me.

As your work gloves hold the shape of your hands as they
await your touch again, so shall you learn to be so patient.

§ 2 §

As you call from afar and the dogs criss-cross back,
exhausted from their wanderings, so might you be thus
called home by a voice larger than your own.

§ 3 §

As the stars reel and brighten above those asleep as well as the watchful ones who are waiting, might I remain always ready to sing, awake or asleep when you find me.

BOUND

FROM A SERIES OF MARKING STONES: BOUND

§ 1 §

Trust is a wish with amnesia.

Insecurity is a form of fishing.

Forgiveness is the blessing one gives oneself.

Friendship is a vessel containing the waters it once sailed across.

§ 2 §

The best friendships sing harmonics to your root note, not your same note.

A troubadour knows fewer people than people who know that troubadour.

People love a troubadour more than a troubadour knows.

People love true labor more than the trouble that comes from idleness.

Trouble can always find a door.

§ 3 §

Jazz darts and dashes around the line of melody as a butterfly flits and floats across the breeze.

A bubble lifts and drifts like love (or vice versa)—it can land on anything, but sometimes pops.

Two bubbles can glance then join as one—a new shared side protected—tumbling in the sun.

True love is neither a bubble nor a song (though they each catch more light as they sail along).

Trouble is merely a shift in the planned route through.

§ 4 §

Curtains become brooms in a breeze.

Sidewalks become mirrors after the rains.

Tears become whatever tears become.

Reasons can shift like light in a room, sometimes quickly if there's a switch.

Certainty allows the mind to walk at its own pace.

§ 5 §

Hard things can be stirred to soften.

The act of blowing can be used to warm (cold hands) or cool (soup).

Kitchens change from empty and cold to full and warm, just like stomachs do.

Bathrooms and bowels work similarly, too.

Politicians can change from full and warm to empty and cold, and are often hard to stomach.

Switches change the flow: pull an alarm, people swarm—like electrons.

Elections change the flow as well: sometimes like bowels, and often more rancid.

Some soft things harden when left to themselves.

§ 6 §

The heart is like a song: it begins and ends with a beat.

The Earth will spin until who knows when.

The end of the Earth may be like a hearth, due to a lack of heart.

"Hearth" begins with heart and ends with earth.

§ 7 §

In the absence of words, silence becomes language.

In the silent turns, a volume to be read.

The hands that turn to the work will assuage the guilt of the idle mind.

The mind that erases criticism, creates a new page for praises ahead.

The danger of ire is the fire of the past destroying the now.

The hunger of jealousy starves the empathy.

In the thirst for new hope, giving becomes water.

In the abundance of laughter, anger is drowned.

In the whispers of the lovers, the future is found.

§ 8 §

A lie is a wish for a different world than this.

A line that is true is what the poet wishes to find.

A poem is a celebration of the world we have, lies and all.

Poets know that words are hard.

A fib is a fable without a moral—until the fib is found out.

Most wishes have something to do the wisher.

Whisperers wish that words not be so hard.

§ 9 §

Crying erases bit by bit.

A smile is a caress from a distance. Shared laughter, a form of embracing.

After the embrace, each side stays lifted where they once sagged.

A sagging gate may scrape and delay, but it clears the path.

Those on the fence are heedless where the fence is weakest.

Those who don't listen wear earplugs and speak the loudest.

Bragging shows at the very least a trace of insecurity, sometimes a surplus.

The confident arrive armed and prepared, and look to avoid a needless fight.

A cold stare is a form of a fist.

A wish is wisdom that the world can be a better place.

A secret betrayed is a kiss laced with poison that harms a confidant on purpose.

Suspicion is a package of pessimism that arrives with postage due.

A letter addressed to yourself shows a belief in your own survival.

§ 10 §

Character is a chain mail suit with a kevlar vest.

Grace is an injured dancer that pirouettes with poise.

Patience is a silence that rides above the noises.

Impatience is an ailing patient pouring the medicine down the drain.

Resistance is a venom that brews its own antidote.

Frustration is just when the focus is too narrow.

Persistence is a slow drip off a spigot wearing a hole in the brick below.

Dishonesty is a kneeling pleader with a trick knee.

Faith is a station whose doors are always open.

A promise is a local train with a schedule to keep.

Trust is the structure you give to another.

§ 11 §

Love at its best is a type of mining where every rock has value.

Happiness is a map that expands all horizons.

Ignorance is a cat that naps on a stovetop.

Patience is a wet match waiting for the clouds to pass.

Honor is a loyal dog that is happy to heel.

Growth is also the belief in it.

Hope is a wish congealed.

Grief is an image on a party balloon that sharpens and contracts as the balloon goes flat, then shrivels to uselessness and never gets tossed aside.

Mourning is the balloon's string, along for the ride.

§ 12 §

Clouds are slow oceans.

Self-consciousness and doubt are rains that shroud emotions.

Pleasure reminds the bereft that there remains a treasure in the chest.

Pain stands up when we lay down.

Chance dances.

Change changes both what is dispelled and what remains.

Fear and boldness balance out when left to the ledgers of dreamtime.

Boredom is a one-note melody played on a dented gong inside one's head.

Dignity is starting again with a grin after tripping or falling.

Regret is the needle on a skipping record, popping off over one glitch again and again.

Happenstance and cacology are words seldom used, whose meanings get confused—each a victim of themselves.

§ 13 §

A kiss is a bridge. Aloneness the chasm.

To connect with one thing
connects one with all that thing
connects with too, which
connects one with all things.

All things connect.
All things change form, become different manifestations
of matter. Therefore,
all things matter.

All things non-matter matter, too
(because all things matter).

§ 14 §

Writers write.

Persistence is the difference between painting one painting and being a painter.

One ski trip does not a skier make, but one fall can break more than vacation plans (including one's will to be a skier).

One heartbreak can break one's heart forever.

Never say never, but sometimes say sometimes.

All of the ways to peel an apple are seen by the knife, but one cut at a time will define the core that remains.

The core of any story holds many seeds.

The road of one-way thinking, while smoothly paved,

misses most of the scenery.

Guide books show merely one route in a web of roads connecting. All roads lead to all roads.

Right and left turns can equal out. Three lefts make a right, three right a left.

Wrongs that are left have to be righted.

Righters right.

§ 15 §

The frame of a doorway differs from the window in more ways than can fit through the door.

More doors exist within a structure than the one or two that lead in. Most doors lead darker lives, then.

Most windows frame views to what's outside. The news of the day arrives through them, whether open or closed. Unlike doors.

Some like doors, but you have to be open to them.

§ 16 §

Every view from the South Pole looks northward.

Every road from the North Pole leads southward.

Every word takes the shape of the mouth that speaks it. Every mouth talks out, gasps in.

The last in line knows there's no one behind them to look to, but at least one unmet friend is standing before them to talk to.

There is more than one way to look at the line of the horizon.

The first to arrive holds the key for all who follow.

Leaders hold doors open for others to walk through.

§ 17 §

Some homes have more doors than necessary.

Some doors are home to more hellos than farewells.

Most wells have echoed more than one "Hello!"

Death is the story continuing on the other side of the door once the traveler has left home.

§ 18 §

Worrying kills the now we are in by filling it with a terrible future, completely imagined— the poison of which is brewed in that very worry.

Regret sacrifices the moment by replaying a terrible past instead. Worry and regret rob this instant from us, force instances of misery, steal from us our happiness.

By thinking elsewhere than where we are, we divide our present, betray the here we have.

§ 19 §

Easy to overpour a full glass. Harder to be poor and give. Frugality with money is seen to be a smart thing, but misers are not wiser. The thirstiest often pour first.

§ 20 §

The liar rides on the scum of betrayal as a bar of soap slides on its dissolving.

The stone skips across the surface, but only a few times before it sinks in, like a cold hard truth repeated by a friend.

§ 21 §

Not succeeding is not the same as failing.
Not caring is the same as failing.
Not trying assures failure.

§ 22 §

Drying a towel is like massaging a masseuse, or teaching a teacher.

Teaching massage involves towels.

Before they contain, containers are shipped in containers.

Containers that nestle in other containers save space. People that nestle in other people create babies.

Another person can save us from throwing our lives away.

It's difficult to throw a trash can away, for the unintentional mixed messages.

Poems can intentionally mix things up to make things clearer, clean us, massage us, teach us, ship us, expand us, save us, and contain the hard to contain.

§ 23 §

When you walk hand in hand, you hold a part of someone who holds a part of yourself.

§ 24 §

Criticism is a gust meant to either bend down or straighten back up.

Praise is a melody that is never loud enough.

Doubt is a whisper that sounds like a shout.

Criticism can arrive hot or cold, burn or chill. Sometimes both.

Melodies are rivers that bend and straighten, bend and straighten.

Rivers are always in the act of straightening. They sing to all that impedes the song of erosion, the way to the sea.

One way to see oneself more clearly is to stop and reflect like still water where the turns are the greatest.

One way to gain elevation is to lift oneself back up, like evaporation.

§ 25 §

Admiring another person is like reading a restaurant menu:

Each is a recognition of things you would eventually like to see in yourself.

Respect and acknowledgment are the keys to good management.

Keys are often issued to good managers, eventually.

Eventually, keys are like combs: each issue shavings of themselves to the locks.

A good athlete is the opposite of a prisoner: one pays one's dues to get locked in when it counts on game day, the other gets locked in and counts the days to pay one's dues.

§ 26 §

Air caught in sleeves at the airport reveals directions: of the wind out on the runway, and of the home of the travelers in the terminal, reaching out for loved ones.

When we point to the stars, we reach out to the unknown.

When we fall in love, we fall into the unknown.

When we fall, we reach out to our future home.

When we imagine the unknown, we reach out with our brains.

We can reach out and reach out, but we can only know a part of this waking life.

When we lay our bodies down, we know the rest.

§ 27 §

As the shadow of the tree falls across the book, the tree finds the shape of what it might become, and the book feels the coldness of the shape of its past.

As the leaves shake from the force of the breeze, they practice the same motions they will repeat once shaken free, and the breeze feels the shape of what it will later carry.

As we carry within the shadow of what's been lost, we shake as if buckling under its weight, as if memory could weigh as much as the thing itself.

As we cast our own shadow behind us, we find the path ahead well lit, and bask in the throw of light across our face, our smile an open book.

§ 28 §

Irregularities in marble are more common than not, thus they are really regularities—and those regular parts are irregularities, then.

Minorities can become majorities simply by becoming more.

We become more when we regularly practice, though practice does not make perfect. Imperfections are perfectly regular in this universe.

If this universe is really a part of many multiverses, it is not a universe then. The multiverses are.

The universe is perfectly perplexing.

§ 29 §

What matters in patterns is repetition. Repetition is what matters in patterns.

Pattern matters are up for debate when analyzing data at demographic meetings. The graphs at demographic meetings could often use better graphics, but static facts matter more to those debating stats than motion graphics do.

When perplexed while debating complex statistics, flexibility is an asset.

Emotion vs. reason is a common battle, always fought in the trenches. Tactics reverse between the heart and head when hand-in-hand becomes hand-to-hand instead.

To question one's answers often answers one's questions.

To doubt what is commonly accepted is uncommon, no doubt about it.

Testing hypotheses can be a bother, but it makes perfect sense to be well versed in it.

To purchase a book of free verse poetry makes it no longer free verse.

§ 30 §

A discarded blouse might understandably fold its arms in disgust, depending on the circumstances of the undressing.

The broken eyeglasses in the bushes may seem to look

askew at the tree branch that broke them.

The old shoes with holes in the soles will eventually get the rest they need.

§ 31 §

If the tongue in the boot could talk, we might learn the history of kicking.

If all hands moved like nurses hands, there would be less pain.

The hands form the work gloves, but the work forms the human.

Feet will stretch the shoes, eventually, but travel quickly expands the mind.

The lines of the hiking trails on the map get traced by fingers more than the actual trails get walked by hiking boots.

Bike wheels are still more than not.

§ 32 §

Drunk people rarely sleep naked. Or strategically.

Pants kicked off sometimes lie on the floor in the same pose as the sleeper who kicked them there.

Clothes shed in pre-sex stripping are rarely hung up.

Sleepers who wear sleepers often fold their day clothes before sleeping (if they don't toss them in the hamper). Some folks fold their clothes for the hamper, too. (Those who do might strategize how to be more spontaneous.)

Folds in sheets can hamper a good night's sleep.

Sex while folded can induce a good night's sleep.

People who talk during sex will say they don't have hang-ups (but might be dreaming).

People who do bootie calls often have hang-ups. And often have hang ups.

Sleep hampers good conversations. Sleep talkers rarely make relevant points (at least not to those not in the dream).

People who dream they are naked in public might fold their hands strategically.

§ 33 §

A rug warms both our feet and the floor beneath.

A coin is warmed more on one side if stored in a pocket.

A coin is worth its face value, face up or face down. That same coin, to a gambler, may be worth more if flipped heads or tails, depending.

A gambler's face can give him away.

A gambler can clean up with a straight.

A gambler who doesn't quit while ahead, customarily goes home with his tail between his legs.

A customer at a store offering giveaways faces long lines at the register, and tired legs and feet.

Old storage given away at curbs might cause neighbors to register frowns on their faces.

The long lines of curbs define front yards.

Gardeners get dirty cleaning up leaves. Front yards are cleaner after gardeners leave.

Leaves straighten in summer, curl and fall in fall.

Rugs, if not straightened, cause people to fall.

Rugs, worn out by feet, curl at curbsides to be given away, just one side warming the pavement beneath.

§ 34 §

Constant is continuous but not continual. Continual has breaks between, so continual is a repeated thing.

Continual is a repeated thing.

"The only constant in life is change" might have been repeated enough to have become trite, but it is no less true.

"'The only constant in life is change' and Other Paradoxes'" might make for a good title, provided it hasn't been used before.

"Paradoxen" might be a better plural for "paradox," based on "ox" and "oxen": As two ox are oxen, a pair of paradoxes are paradoxen.

Trite is cliché, but some trite things are not of little import. Just well-worn.

Salt granules are little imports.

Old sailors are salts. Old sayings are saws.

Old sailors are well-worn, and some are worn out.

Some old saws are rusty, both the tools and the sayings.

Old tools are thrown out. Old sayings, too, until they become platitudes. Then they are thrown out (as in thrown away). Like old chestnuts.

§ 35 §

Successful recipes call for seasoning to taste.

Colder seasons call for soup.

The chef chopping onions salts the broth with tears.

Tears in the cloth ignore the faultline of the seam.

Those at fault often ignore the tears they cause.

A frayed edge frees the thread.

A thread of thought can sew a coat of ideas.

Those who are ignorant stay naked and afraid.

Ideas create new recipes for success.

§ 36 §

Conscience is the memory of light affecting choices.

Character, like shadow, is defined by degree of alignment with the source of light.

Reputation is the history of choices aligned.

Revelation is a match struck in a dark room.

Metaphors for insight using "light" are often trite.

Good advice, like lightning, gifts a new path to be followed, ghosted across one's line of sight.

A good line can spark and sparkle the eyes.

A good poem is a flashlight, leading the eye to what had been missed in the world beyond the obvious.

A good book is a floodlight.

Literature remembered becomes an inner torch.

Learning can be a light rain or a storm, depending.

The blind spots of our ignorance are parched crops.

Our sharing of stories together is both the harvest and the sowing.

Our ingesting of each other's wisdom is also our own knowing.

§ 37 §

A door is an exception to a wall.

A window in a door is far better traveled than the average window, even if only within one room. Windows in cars and planes are the bon vivants of the glass family.

Double-paned windows are a pain to clean if dust gets stuck in between.

Pain offers a window to character, revealing what's inside by how one reacts.

One's character hinges on one's actions.

The action of a door hinge depends on friction.

Hinges, unlike humans, have just one degree of freedom.

§ 38 §

One may try to succeed, but moreso one succeeds by trying.

§ 39 §

Religions are guesses of plot twists that await us after the curtain comes down.

The grieving faithful clap madly in the dark, await the encore that might never come.

§ 40 §

Faith:

Tickets purchased in advance.

(Pitons hammered into cracks, high on a cliff face wall.)

§ 41 §

Harvest:

A smile lifted by a glance.

(The painter's painting, rendered flawlessly after a lifetime of practice and learning.)

§ 42 §

Ignorance:

Saying to the painter: "Oh, you're so lucky. I'm just not naturally gifted like you are."

(A loose tongue that runs like a broken spigot, flooding the house with news about that tongue's owner.)

§ 43 §

Betrayal:

A promise spoken and forgotten that later leaves a true friend confused and waiting.

(The faintest feign that send the dog running after the not tossed ball.)

§ 44 §

A dream is a bird asleep that does not comprehend its nest.

§ 45 §

Gratitude is the first flight, with beak still held open to the sky.

§ 46 §

Hunger is the hinge on the jaw that keeps us singing.

ACKNOWLEDGMENTS

Thanks to

my family,

my friends,

my students,

my colleagues,

my poetry communities.

Thanks to Mark Givens and Pelekinesis.

Thanks to "this vast similitude" that spans and encloses.

ABOUT THE AUTHOR

Grant Hier was appointed as the inaugural Poet Laureate of Anaheim in 2018. His long poem, *Untended Garden: Histories and Reinhabitation in Suburbia*, was awarded Prize Americana in 2014, published as a book by Poetry Press the following year, and subsequently nominated for both an American Book Award and the Kate Tufts Discovery Award. His poetry collection *The Difference Between* (Pelekinesis) was published in April of 2018, to which *Similitude* is a companion collection. A book of historical flash fiction, *California Continuum: Migrations and Amalgamations*, which was co-written with the Poet Laureate of Sequoia and Kings Canyon Parks, John Brantingham, is forthcoming in February, 2019 (also on Pelekinesis). Grant has previously been awarded the Nancy Dew Taylor Prize for Literary Excellence in Poetry and the Kick Prize for poetry. His writing has been anthologized in such books as *Only Light Can Do That* (Rattling Wall/ PEN Center USA), *Monster Verse—Human and Inhuman Poems* (Knopf/Everyman), *Orange County: A Literary Field Guide* (Heyday), *LA Fiction Anthology* (Red Hen), and *John Fante: A Critical Gathering* (Fairleigh Dickinson University Press). In addition to writing, he is a musical artist, visual artist, and former graphic designer and art director. As a voice actor, he contributed to the audio book of George Saunders' *Lincoln in the Bardo*, which won the 2018 Audie Award for Audiobook of the year. Grant is a Full Professor at Laguna College of Art and Design where he teaches a variety of Liberal Arts classes, including creative writing. More at www.granthier.com

www.ingramcontent.com/pod-product-compliance
Lightning Source LLC
Chambersburg PA
CBHW020930090426
42736CB00010B/1095